THE HUNT BY NIGHT

DEREK MAHON

The Hunt by Night

OXFORD UNIVERSITY PRESS

1982

Oxford University Press, Walton Street, Oxford OX2 6DP

London Glasgow New York Toronto
Delhi Bombay Calcutta Madras Karachi
Kuala Lumpur Singapore Hong Kong Tokyo
Nairobi Dar es Salaam Cape Town
Melbourne Auckland

and associates in
Beirut Berlin Ibadan Mexico City Nicosia

This edition is not for sale in the
United States of America

British Library Cataloguing in Publication Data
Mahon, Derek
The hunt by night.
I. Title
821'.914   PR6063.A/
ISBN 0-19-211953-2

Set by Rowland Phototypesetting Ltd
Printed in Great Britain by
J. W. Arrowsmith Ltd
Bristol

TO THE MEMORY
OF
J. G. FARRELL
1935–1979

Acknowledgements

Acknowledgements are due to *The Times Literary Supplement, The London Review of Books, The New Statesman, The Listener, Encounter, Quarto, The London Magazine, New Poetry, The Poetry Review, Aquarius, The New Edinburgh Review, The Honest Ulsterman, The Irish Times, New Irish Writing, The Poetry Ireland Review, Ploughshares* (Cambridge, Mass.) and *New World Journal* (Berkeley, Ca.); and to the BBC and RTE. 'How to Live' and 'A Lighthouse in Maine' first appeared in *The Hudson Review*. Thanks are also due to Gallery Books, Dublin; to the Irish Academy of Letters; and to the Arts Council of Great Britain.

Contents

Courtyards in Delft   9
Derry Morning   11
North Wind: Portrush   12
An Old Lady   14
Rathlin Island   16
Brecht in Svendborg   17
Knut Hamsun in Old Age   20
The Andean Flute   22
At the Pool   23
Tractatus   23
Morning Radio   24
Rock Music   25
The Dawn Chorus   26
Table Talk   27
Another Sunday Morning   28
The Hunt by Night   30
Girls on the Bridge   32
Brighton Beach   34
How to Live   36
Ovid in Tomis   37
A Lighthouse in Maine   43
The Joycentenary Ode   45
A Postcard from Berlin   49
One of these Nights   50
The Terminal Bar   52
from The Drunken Boat   53
A Garage in Co. Cork   55
The Woods   57
The Earth   59
The Globe in North Carolina   61

Courtyards in Delft

– PIETER DE HOOCH, 1659

(for Gordon Woods)

Oblique light on the trite, on brick and tile –
Immaculate masonry, and everywhere that
Water tap, that broom and wooden pail
To keep it so. House-proud, the wives
Of artisans pursue their thrifty lives
Among scrubbed yards, modest but adequate.
Foliage is sparse, and clings. No breeze
Ruffles the trim composure of those trees.

No spinet-playing emblematic of
The harmonies and disharmonies of love;
No lewd fish, no fruit, no wide-eyed bird
About to fly its cage while a virgin
Listens to her seducer, mars the chaste
Precision of the thing and the thing made.
Nothing is random, nothing goes to waste:
We miss the dirty dog, the fiery gin.

That girl with her back to us who waits
For her man to come home for his tea
Will wait till the paint disintegrates
And ruined dykes admit the esurient sea;
Yet this is life too, and the cracked
Out-house door a verifiable fact
As vividly mnemonic as the sunlit
Railings that front the houses opposite.

I lived there as a boy and know the coal
Glittering in its shed, late-afternoon
Lambency informing the deal table,
The ceiling cradled in a radiant spoon.
I must be lying low in a room there,
A strange child with a taste for verse,
While my hard-nosed companions dream of war
On parched veldt and fields of rain-swept gorse;

For the pale light of that provincial town
Will spread itself, like ink or oil,
Over the not yet accurate linen
Map of the world which occupies one wall
And punish nature in the name of God.
If only, now, the Maenads, as of right,
Came smashing crockery, with fire and sword,
We could sleep easier in our beds at night.

Derry Morning

The mist clears and the cavities
Glow black in the rubbled city's
Broken mouth. An early crone,
Muse of a fitful revolution
Wasted by the fray, she sees
Her *aisling* falter in the breeze,
Her oak-grove vision hesitate
By empty wharf and city gate.

Here it began, and here at least
It fades into the finite past
Or seems to: clattering shadows whop
Mechanically over pub and shop.
A strangely pastoral silence rules
The shining roofs and murmuring schools;
For this is how the centuries work –
Two steps forward, one step back.

Hard to believe this tranquil place,
Its desolation almost peace,
Was recently a boom-town wild
With expectation, each unscheduled
Incident a measurable
Tremor on the Richter Scale
Of world events, each vibrant scene
Translated to the drizzling screen.

What of the change envisioned here,
The quantum leap from fear to fire?
Smoke from a thousand chimneys strains
One way beneath the returning rains
That shroud the bomb-sites, while the fog
Of time receives the ideologue.
A Russian freighter bound for home
Mourns to the city in its gloom.

North Wind: Portrush

I shall never forget the wind
On this benighted coast.
It works itself into the mind
Like the high keen of a lost
Lear-spirit in agony
Condemned for eternity

To wander cliff and cove
Without comfort, without love.
It whistles off the stars
And the existential, black
Face of the cosmic dark:
We crouch to roaring fires.

Yet there are mornings when,
Even in midwinter, sunlight
Flares, and a rare stillness
Lies upon roof and garden,
Each object eldritch-bright,
The sea scarred but at peace.

Then, from the ship we say
Is the lit town where we live
(Our whiskey-and-forecast world),
A smaller ship that sheltered
All night in the restless bay
Will weigh anchor and leave.

What did they think of us
During their brief sojourn?
A string of lights on the prom
Dancing mad in the storm –
Who lives in such a place?
And will they ever return?

But the shops open at nine
As they have always done,
The wrapped-up bourgeoisie
Hardened by wind and sea.
The newspapers are late
But the milk shines in its crate.

Everything swept so clean
By tempest, wind and rain!
Elated, you might believe
That this was the first day –
A false sense of reprieve,
For the climate is here to stay.

So best prepare for the worst
That chaos and old night
Can do to us. Were we not
Raised on such expectations,
Our hearts starred with frost
Through countless generations?

Elsewhere the olive grove,
Le déjeuner sur l'herbe,
Poppies and parasols,
Blue skies and mythic love.
Here only the stricken souls
No spring can unperturb.

Prospero and his people never
Came to these stormy parts:
Few do who have the choice.
Yet, blasting the subtler arts,
That weird, plaintive voice
Choirs now and for ever.

An Old Lady

The old motorbike she was
The first woman in those
Parts to ride – a noble
Norton – disintegrates
With rusty iron gates
In some abandoned stable;

But lives in sepia shades
Where an emancipated
Country schoolteacher
Of nineteen thirty-eight
Grins from her frame before
Broaching the mountain roads.

Forty years later she
Shakes slack on the fire
To dowse it while she goes
Into the town to buy
Groceries and newspaper
And exchange courtesies.

Then back to a pot of tea
And the early-evening news
(Some fresh atrocity);
Washes up to the sound
Of a chat-show, one phrase
Of Bach going round and round

In her head as she stares
Out at the wintry moon
And thinks of her daughters
So very far away –
Although the telephone
Makes nonsense of that today.

Out there beyond the edge
Of the golf course tosses
The ghost of the *Girona*,
Flagship of the Armada –
History. Does the knowledge
Alter the world she sees?

Or do her thoughts travel
By preference among
Memories of her naval
Husband, thirty years
Drowned, the watercolours
And instruments unstrung?

A tentatively romantic
Figure once, she became
Merely an old lady like
Many another, with
Her favourite programme
And her sustaining faith.

She sits now and watches
Incredulously as some mad
Whipper-snapper howls
His love-song and the gulls
Snuggle down on the beaches,
The rooks in the churchyard.

Rathlin Island

A long time since the last scream cut short –
Then an unnatural silence; and then
A natural silence, slowly broken
By the shearwater, by the sporadic
Conversation of crickets, the bleak
Reminder of a metaphysical wind.
Ages of this, till the report
Of an outboard motor at the pier
Fractures the dream-time, and we land
As if we were the first visitors here.

The whole island a sanctuary where amazed
Oneiric species whistle and chatter,
Evacuating rock-face and cliff-top.
Cerulean distance, an oceanic haze –
Nothing but sea-smoke to the ice-cap
And the odd somnolent freighter.
Bombs doze in the housing estates
But here they are through with history –
Custodians of a lone light that repeats
One simple statement to the turbulent sea.

A long time since the unspeakable violence –
Since Somhairle Buidh, powerless on the mainland,
Heard the screams of the Rathlin women
Borne to him, seconds after, upon the wind.
Only the cry of the shearwater
And the roar of the outboard motor
Disturb the singular peace. Spray-blind,
We leave here the infancy of the race,
Unsure among the pitching surfaces
Whether the future lies before us or behind.

Brecht in Svendborg

I *A Danish Refuge*

We have lashed oars on the thatch
To keep it down in everything
Short of a cyclone, and
The sun gilds our garden;
But deadly visions hang
Like rain-clouds in the sound.

A little boat with a patched
Sail skates on the crinkly
Tinfoil of the bay; but we
Are not deceived by scenery.
Ears cocked, we can hear
Screams beyond the frontier.

The owl announces death
From the foliage these spring
Nights while I read *Macbeth*,
Kant, or the *Tao Tê Ching*;
Twice daily the starlings
Are silenced by a shriek

Of ordnance from the naval
War-games of the Reich.
The whitewash is peeling
From the damp ceiling
As I work at *Galileo*
In the converted stable.

Tacked to the oak beams,
A stage poster from
The old Schiffbauerdamm,
Faded now, proclaims
THE TRUTH IS CONCRETE.
Confucius' scroll portrait,

The ashtrays, cigar boxes
And drawers of microfilm
Make everything familiar.
From here I can watch
Helene gardening,
The children at the swing.

This could be home from home
If things were otherwise.
Twice daily the mails come
Up the sound in a ship.
I notice that the house
Has four doors for escape . . .

2   *To the Unborn*

Truly, we live in a dark time.
The candid word is suicide;
A clear brow argues
A thick skin. The man
Who laughs is merely someone
Who has not yet heard the terrible news.

What sort of times are these
When idle chat is treated
As wicked nonsense,
Implying as it does
Avoidance of other topics?
And who has a clear conscience?

Eat, drink and be thankful! –
But how can I do this
If my food belongs
To the starving,
My drink to the parched?
At the same time, I eat and drink.

I would so much like to be wise,
To shun strife and live
Quietly, without fear;
To love my enemies.
I can do none of these.
Truly, we live in a dark time.

We know that hatred, even of evil,
Disfigures the face;
That anger, even at cruelty,
Hardens the voice.
We who wished to found
A kind future could not ourselves be kind.

To the unborn who will emerge
From the deluge
In which we drown
I would say only this:
Remember, when you condemn us,
You do not live, like us, in a dark time.

Startled awake at first light
By whistling, I peer out
At the garden, where a young
Fellow in torn denims
Is cheerfully pocketing plums.
He nods to me and returns to his song.

Knut Hamsun in Old Age

While a late thaw began in the boarded eaves
I left, exhausted, that city nobody leaves
Without being marked by it; signed on
For Newcastle-upon-Tyne and so to Spain,
Renouncing the tightly corseted lives,
The many windows flashing in the sun.
Dream on, dream homes, until I come again!

Later the wives and the hard-earned estate,
The admiration of the acknowledged great;
But who could hope wholly to sublimate
The bad years, the imperious gratitude
Working like hunger at the very bone?
And so, my larder dim with surplus food,
My polished windows blazing in the sun,

Waking, these days, I sometimes think myself
Back in that attic with its empty shelf.
Strangely enough, it was enormous fun
Glaring, a madman, into the bun faces
Of outraged butchers and policemen
And acting the idiot in public places:
The conquering soul betrayed a manic grin.

Born of the earth, I made terms with the earth,
This being the only thing of lasting worth.
Beside my bed the dog-eared gods of art
Made way for fragrant works on crop rotation,
The agriculture where all cultures start.
The typewriter fell silent; rod and gun
Went out with me to prowl the watchful dawn.

Yes, I shook hands with Hitler; knew disgrace.
But time heals everything; I rose again.
Now I can look my butcher in the face.
Besides, did I not once, as a young man,
Cure myself of incipient tuberculosis
Inhaling four sub-zero nights and days
Perched on the screaming roof of a freight train?

One fortunate in both would have us choose
'Perfection of the life or of the work'.
Nonsense, you work best on a full stomach
As everybody over thirty knows –
For who, unbreakfasted, will love the lark?
Prepare your protein-fed epiphanies,
Your heavenly mansions blazing in the dark.

The Andean Flute

He dances to that music in the wood
As if history were no more than a dream.
Who said the banished gods were gone for good?

The furious rhythm creates a manic mood,
Piercing the twilight like a mountain stream.
He dances to that music in the wood.

We might have put on Bach or Buxtehude,
But a chance impulse chose the primal scream.
Who said the banished gods were gone for good?

An Inca frenzy fires his northern blood.
His child-heart picking up the tribal beam,
He dances to that music in the wood.

A puff of snow bursts where the birches brood;
Along the lane the earliest snowdrops gleam.
Who said the banished gods were gone for good?

It is the ancient cry for warmth and food
That moves him. Acting out an ancient theme,
He dances to that music in the wood.
Who said the banished gods were gone for good?

At the Pool

My four-year-old daughter
points up at the low
ceiling with a cry:
'Look at the shadow
of the water on the sky!'

Tractatus

(for Aidan Higgins)

'The world is everything that is the case'
From the fly giving up in the coal-shed
To the Winged Victory of Samothrace.
Give blame, praise, to the fumbling God
Who hides, shame-facèdly, His agèd face;
Whose light retires behind its veil of cloud.

The world, though, is also so much more –
Everything that is the case imaginatively.
Tacitus believed mariners could *hear*
The sun sinking into the western sea;
And who would question that titanic roar,
The steam rising wherever the edge may be?

Morning Radio

(for John Scotney)

The silence of the ether . . .
What can be going on
In the art-nouveau liner?

Ah, now the measured pips,
A stealth of strings
Tickling the fretwork throat,

Woodwinds entering
Delicately, the clarinet
Ascending to a lark-like note.

Seven o'clock –
News-time, and the merciful
Voice of Tom Crowe

Explains with sorrow
That the world we know
Is coming to an end.

Even as he speaks
We can hear furniture
Creak and slide on the decks.

But first a brief recital
Of resonant names –
Mozart, Schubert, Brahms.

The sun shines,
And a new day begins
To the strains of a horn concerto.

Rock Music

The ocean glittered quietly in the moonlight
While heavy metal rocked the discotheques;
Space-age Hondas farted half the night,
Fired by the prospect of fortuitous sex.
I sat late at the window, bland with rage,
And listened to the tumult down below,
Trying to concentrate on the printed page
As if such obsolete bumf could save us now.

Next morning, wandering on the strand, I heard
Left-over echoes of the night before
Dwindle to echoes, and a single bird
Drown with a whistle that residual roar.
Rock music started up on every side –
Whisper of algae, click of stone on stone,
A thousand limpets left by the ebb-tide
Unanimous in their silent inquisition.

The Dawn Chorus

It is not sleep itself but dreams we miss,
Say the psychologists; and the poets too.
We yearn for that reality in this.

The soul, said Samuel Palmer, is a chrysalis
Dreaming of wings (of Shoreham bathed in blue).
It is not sleep itself but dreams we miss.

If we could once achieve a synthesis
Of the archaic and the entirely new . . .
We yearn for that reality in this.

But, wide awake, clear-eyed with cowardice,
The flaming seraphim we find untrue.
It is not sleep itself but dreams we miss.

Listening heart-broken to the dawn chorus,
Clutching the certainty that once we flew,
We yearn for that reality in this.

Awaiting still our metamorphosis,
We hoard the fragments of what once we knew.
It is not sleep itself but dreams we miss.
We yearn for that reality in this.

Table Talk

You think I am your servant but you are wrong –
The service lies with you. During your long
Labours at me, I am the indulgent wood,
Tolerant of your painstaking ineptitude.
Your poems were torn from me by violence;
I am here to receive your homage in dark silence.

Remembering the chain-saw surgery and the seaward groan,
Like a bound and goaded exodus from Babylon,
I pray for a wood-spirit to make me dance,
To scare you shitless and upset your balance,
Destroy the sedate poise with which you pour
Forth your ephemeral stream of literature.

When I was a pine and lived in a cold climate
I listened to leaf-rumours about our fate;
But I have come a long way since then
To watch the sun glint on your reflective pen.
The hurt I do resent, and my consolation
Will be the unspoilt paper when you have gone.

And yet I love you, even in your ignorance,
Perhaps because at last you are making sense –
Talking to me, not through me, recognizing
That it is I alone who let you sing
Wood music. Hitherto shadowy and dumb,
I speak to you now as your indispensable medium.

Another Sunday Morning

We wake and watch the sun make bright
The corners of our London flat –
No sound but the sporadic, surly
Snarl of a car making an early
Dash for the country or the coast.
This is the time I like the most
When, for an hour or two, the strife
And strain of the late bourgeois life

Let up, we lie and grin to hear
The children bickering next door –
Hilarious formulations based
On a weird logic we have lost.
Oil crises and vociferous crowds
Seem as far off as tiny clouds;
The long-range forecast prophesies
Mean temperatures and azure skies.

Out in the park where Celia's father
Died, the Sunday people gather –
Residents towed by Afghan hounds,
Rastafarians trailing 'sounds',
Provincial tourists, Japanese
Economists, Saudi families,
Fresh-faced American college kids
Making out in the green shades.

A chiliastic prig, I prowl
Among the dog-lovers and growl;
Among the kite-fliers and fly
The private kite of poetry –
A sort of winged sandwich board
El-Grecoed to receive the Lord;
An airborne, tremulous brochure
Proclaiming that the end is near.

Black diplomats with stately wives,
Sauntering by, observe the natives
Dozing beside the palace gates –
Old ladies under wide straw-hats
Who can remember *Chu Chin Chow*
And Kitchener. Exhausted now
By decades of retrenchment, they
Wait for the rain at close of play.

So many empires come and gone –
The spear and scimitar laid down,
The long-bow and the arquebus
Adapted to domestic use.
A glimpse of George V at Cowes
Lives on behind the wrinkled brows
Of an old man in Bognor Regis
Making dreadnoughts out of matches.

Asia now for a thousand years –
A flower that blooms and disappears
In a sand-storm; every artefact
A pure, self-referential act,
That the intolerant soul may be
Retrieved from triviality
And the locked heart, so long in pawn
To steel, redeemed by wood and stone.

The Hunt by Night

— UCCELLO, 1465

Flickering shades,
Stick figures, lithe game,
Swift flights of bison in a cave
Where man the maker killed to live;
But neolithic bush became
The midnight woods

Of nursery walls,
The ancient fears mutated
To play, horses to rocking-horses
Tamed and framed to courtly uses,
Crazed no more by foetid
Bestial howls

But rampant to
The pageantry they share
And echoes of the hunting horn
At once peremptory and forlorn.
The mild herbaceous air
Is lemon-blue,

The glade aglow
With pleasant mysteries,
Diuretic depots, pungent prey;
And midnight hints at break of day
Where, among sombre trees,
The slim dogs go

Wild with suspense
Leaping to left and right,
Their cries receding to a point
Masked by obscurities of paint –
As if our hunt by night,
So very tense,

So long pursued,
In what dark cave begun
And not yet done, were not the great
Adventure we suppose but some elaborate
Spectacle put on for fun
And not for food.

Girls on the Bridge

– MUNCH, 1900

Audible trout,
Notional midges. Beds,
Lamplight and crisp linen, wait
In the house there for the sedate
Limbs and averted heads
Of the girls out

Late on the bridge.
The dusty road that slopes
Past is perhaps the main road south,
A symbol of world-wondering youth,
Of adolescent hopes
And privileges;

But stops to find
The girls content to gaze
At the unplumbed, reflective lake,
Their plangent conversational quack
Expressive of calm days
And peace of mind.

Grave daughters
Of time, you lightly toss
Your hair as the long shadows grow
And night begins to fall. Although
Your laughter calls across
The dark waters,

A ghastly sun
Watches in pale dismay.
Oh, you may laugh, being as you are
Fair sisters of the evening star,
But wait – if not today
A day will dawn

When the bad dreams
You hardly know will scatter
The punctual increment of your lives.
The road resumes, and where it curves,
A mile from where you chatter,
Somebody screams . . .

Brighton Beach

(for Paul Smyth)

I

Remember those awful parties
In dreary Belfast flats,
The rough sectarian banter
Of Lavery's back bar,
The boisterous take-aways
And moonlight on wet slates?

Remember the place you rented
At the end of a muddy lane
Somewhere near Muckamore?
No light, so in midwinter
You went to bed at four
And lay there until dawn.

Remember the time we drove
To Donegal and you talked
For hours to fishermen
You had worked with, while I,
Out of my depth in these
Waters, loafed on the quays?

Now, pushing forty, we roam
At ease along the prom,
Life-buffeted to be sure
But grown sober and wise.
The sea shuffles ashore
Beneath pale mackerel skies.

2

From the far end of the pier
I imagine the sun-gleam
On a thousand *deux-chevaux*.
Over there they explore
Balbec and sip Pernod
In a Monet-monoxide dream.

Europe thrives, but the off-shore
Islanders year by year
Decline, the spirit of empire
Fugitive as always.
Now, in this rancorous peace,
Should come the spirit of place.

Too late, though, for already
Places as such are dead
Or nearly; the loved sea
Reflects banality.
Not so in the old days
The retired sailor says.

But the faded Georgian bricks
Towering over the shore
Remain, like the upright
Old men with walking-sticks
Out for a last stroll before
Turning in for the night.

How to Live

(Horace, *Odes*, Book One, 11)

Don't waste your time, Leuconoé, living in fear
    and hope
of the imprevisable future; forget the horoscope.
Accept whatever happens. Whether the gods allow
us fifty winters more or drop us at this one now
which flings the high Tyrrhenian waves on the
    stone piers,
decant your wine: the days are more fun than
    the years
which pass us by while we discuss them. Act with
    zest
one day at a time, and never mind the rest.

Ovid in Tomis

What coarse god
Was the gear-box in the rain
Beside the road?

What nereid the unsinkable
Hair conditioner
Knocking the icy rocks?

They stare me out
With the chaste gravity
And feral pride

Of noble savages
Set down
On an alien shore.

It is so long
Since my own transformation
Into a stone,

I often forget
That there was a time
Before my name

Was mud in the mouths
Of the Danube,
A dirty word in Rome.

Imagine Byron banished
To Botany Bay
Or Wilde to Dawson City

And you have some idea
How it is for me
On the shores of the Black Sea.

I who once strode
Head-high in the forum,
A living legend,

Fasten my sheepskin
By greasy waters
In a Scythian wind.

My wife and friends
Do what they can
On my behalf.

From young Tiberius,
Whom God preserve,
I expect nothing;

But I don't want
To die here
In the back of beyond

Among these morose
Dice-throwing Getes
And the dust of Thrace.

No doubt, in time
To come, this huddle of
Mud huts will be

A handsome city,
An important port,
A popular resort,

With an oil pipeline,
Martini terraces
And even a dignified

Statue of *me*
Gazing out to sea
From the promenade;

But for the moment
It is merely a place
Where I have to be.

Six years now
Since my relegation
To this town

By the late Augustus.
The *Halieutica*,
However desultory,

Gives me a sense
Of purpose,
However factitious;

But I think it's the birds
That please me most,
The cranes and pelicans.

I often sit in the dunes
Listening hard
To the uninhibited

Virtuosity of a lark
Serenading the sun
And meditate upon

The transience
Of earthly dominion,
The perfidy of princes.

Mediocrity, they say,
Consoles itself
With the reflection

That genius so often
Comes to a bad end.
The things adversity

Teaches us
About human nature
As the aphorisms strike home!

I know the simple life
Would be right for me
If I were a simple man.

I have a real sense
Of the dumb spirit
In boulder and tree:

Skimming stones, I wince
With vicarious pain
As a slim quoit goes in.

And the six-foot reeds
Of the delta,
The pathos there!

Whenever they bend
And sigh in the wind
It is not merely Syrinx

Rembering Syrinx
But Syrinx keening
Her naked terror

Of the certain future,
She and her kind
Being bulk-destined

For the pulping machines
And the cording
Of motor-car tyres.

Pan is dead, and already
I feel an ancient
Unity leave the earth,

The bowl avoid my eye
As if ashamed
Of my failure to keep faith.

(It knows that I
Have exchanged belief
For documentation.)

The Muse is somewhere
Else, not here
By this frozen lake –

Or, if here, then I am
Not poet enough
To make the connection.

Are we truly alone
With our physics and myths,
The stars no more

Than glittering dust,
With no one there
To hear our choral odes?

If so, we can start
To ignore the silence
Of infinite space

And concentrate instead
On the infinity
Under our very noses –

The cry at the heart
Of the artichoke,
The gaiety of atoms.

Better to contemplate
The blank page
And leave it blank

Than modify
Its substance by
So much as a pen-stroke.

Woven of wood-nymphs,
It speaks volumes
No one will ever write.

I incline my head
To its candour
And weep for our exile.

A Lighthouse in Maine

It might be anywhere,
That ivory tower
Approached by a dirt road.

Bleached stone against
Bleached sky, it faces
Every way with an air

Of squat omniscience –
A polished Buddha
Hard and bright beyond

Vegetable encroachment.
The north light
That strikes its frame

Houses is not
The light of heaven
But that of this world;

Nor is its task
To throw a punctual
Glow in the dark

To liners wild
With rock music and calm
With navigation.

Though built to shed
Light, it prefers
To shelter it, as it does

Now in the one-bird hour
Of afternoon, a milky
Glare melting the telephone poles.

It works both ways,
Of course, light
Being, like love and the cold,

Something that you
Can give and keep
At the same time.

Night and day it sits
Above the ocean like
A kindly eye, keeping

And giving the rainbow
Of its many colours,
Each of them white.

It might be anywhere –
Hokkaido, Normandy, Maine;
But it is in Maine.

You make a right
Somewhere beyond Rockland,
A left, a right,

You turn a corner and
There it is, shining
In modest glory like

The soul of Adonais.
Out you get and
Walk the rest of the way.

The Joycentenary Ode

Aged twenty-odd, I spent
A night stretched
Between blankets on

The cold floor
Of your squat tower,
Gymsoul, my ho head heavy

As yonder stone among
Half-empty rosbif
And electricity glasses.

There I dreamed
The wholething from
Once upon a time

To riverrun, from
Creak of dawn
To crack of doom,

And woke to find
The snotgreen glittering
Like razor-blades.

What can I tale you,
Jerms, where you stretch
In the Flutherin Symatery?

What pome of mine might
Healp aliviate
Youretournal night?

What news of the warld
You loft bihand
Widdamuse you now?

The goodguise bate
The badgoys in
Diturrible fright

That drove you from
Parease to die
In switzocclusion.

Women no longer run
Panting into cake-shops,
Though we have still

To instal emergency
Phones in coffins
As you proposed.

Everbaddy reads
Your wooks now in
Unlimited eruditions;

And if you never won
The Noble Praise,
Well, that reflects upon

Our precontraceptions
About lutherature, and erges
Your origeniosity.

Gemsbounder has replaced
Hopalongcarcity
At the Pavlodeograph;

The pap democrisy
You realised has become
Thanew art forrum.

Spundrawers in every
Kirtschen! Airwickers
In ivery bahrfrheum!

A noddindog in the rear
Winda of avery carr!
A bonne in overy hoven!

The bairdboard
Bombardment screen
And gineral californucation

Have revolationized
Ourland beyond raggednition.
Nialson came down

A tunderish clap,
Aye-eye in the dust;
And soon there will be

Anew ring-roarrrd built
On reclaimed land
Offa Sandymount Strand.

But some things change
So slowly they
Are still there when

Time comes round again,
Like the dark rain
Muttering on the grave

Of the consumptive
Boy from the gas-works
Who died for love.

Gazing wist, folden
Gavriels, childers of leidt,
We cmome to a place

Beyond cumminity
Where only the wind synges.
Words faoil there

Bifar infunity,
One evenereal stare
Twintwinkling on the si.

This is the dark adge
Where the souil swails
With hurtfealt soang,

Hearing the sonerous
Volapuke of the waives,
That ainchant tongue,

Dialect of what thribe,
Throb of what broken heart –
A language beyond art

That not even you,
If you lived
To a hundred and wan,
Could begin to danscribe.

A Postcard from Berlin

(for Paul Durcan)

We know the cities by their stones
Where Ararat flood-water shines
And violets have struggled through
The bloody dust. Skies are the blue
Of postcard skies, and the leaves green
In that quaint quarter of Berlin.
Wool-gatheringly, the clouds migrate:
No checkpoint checks their tenuous flight.

I hear echoes of Weimar tunes,
Grosz laughter in the beer-gardens
Of a razed Reich, and rumbling tyres
Unter den Linden; but the fires
Of abstract rage, exhausted there,
Blaze out of control elsewhere –
Perhaps one reason you pursue
This night-hunt with no end in view.

I can imagine your dismay
As, cornered in some zinc café,
You read of another hunger-strike,
A postman blasted off his bike . . .
Oh, Hölderlin no fly would hurt,
Our vagabond and pilgrim spirit,
Give us a ring on your way back
And tell us what the nations lack!

One of these Nights

A pregnant moon of August
Composes the roof-tops'
Unventilated slopes;
Dispenses to the dust
Its milky balm. A blue
Buzzard blinks in the zoo.

Cashel and Angkor Wat
Are not more ghostly than
London now, its squares
Bone-pale in the moonlight,
Its quiet thoroughfares
A map of desolation.

The grime of an ephemeral
Culture is swept clean
By that celestial hoover,
The refuse of an era
Consumed like cellophane
In its impartial glare.

A train trembles deep
In the earth; vagrants sleep
Beside the revolving doors
Of vast department stores
Past whose alarm systems
The moonlight blandly streams.

A breeze-ruffled news-stand
Headlines the dole queues,
The bleak no-longer-news
Of racism and inflation –
Straws in the rising wind
That heralds the cyclone.

It all happened before –
The Road to Wigan Pier,
The long road from Jarrow
To the tea-room at the Ritz;
Munich, the Phony War,
The convoys and the Blitz.

One of these nights quiescent
Sirens will start to go
– A dog-howl reminiscent
Of forty years ago –
And sleepy people file
Down to the shelters while

Radiant warplanes come
Droning up the Thames from
Gravesend to Blackfriars,
Westminster and Mayfair,
Their incandescent flowers
Unfolding everywhere.

Next time will be the last –
But, safe in the underground
With tea and *Picture Post*,
We'll take out the guitar
And pass the gaspers round
The way we did before;
And life will begin once more.

The Terminal Bar

(for Philip Haas)

The television set hung
in its wire-net cage,
protected from the flung
bottle of casual rage,
is fetish and icon
providing all we want
of magic and redemption,
routine and sentiment.
The year-old tinsels hang
where an unclaimed no-hoper
trembles; fly-corpses cling
to the grimy fly-paper.
Manhattan snows swarm
on constellated waters,
steam trails from warm
subway ventilators . . .
Welcome to the planet,
its fluorescent beers
buzzing in the desolate
silence of the spheres.
Slam the door and knock
the snow from your shoe,
admit that the vast dark
at last defeated you –
nobody found the grail
or conquered outer space.
Join the clientele
watching itself increase.

from *The Drunken Boat*

(after Rimbaud)

Hearing the thunder of the intransitive weirs,
I felt my guiding tow-ropes slacken; crazed
Apaches, yelping, nailed my gondoliers
Naked to stakes where fiery feathers blazed.

Not that I cared. Relieved of the dull weight
Of cautious crew and inventoried cargo –
Phlegmatic flax, quotidian grain – I let
The current carry me where I chose to go.

Deaf to the furious whisperings of the sand,
My heart rose to a tidal detonation;
Peninsulas, ripped screaming from the land,.
Crashed in a stinging mist of exultation.

Storms smiled on my salt sea-morning sleep.
I danced, light as a cork, nine nights or more
Upon the intractable, man-trundling deep,
Contemptuous of the blinking lights ashore.

Juice of the oceans, tart as unripe fruit,
Burst on my spruce boards in tongues of brine
That tore the spinning binnacle from its root,
Rinsing the curdled puke and the blue wine.

Thenceforth I was submerged in a sea-poem
Infused with milky stars, gulped the profound
Viridian where, disconsolate and calm,
Rapt faces drifted past of the long drowned.

I saw skies split by lightning, granite waves
Shaking the earth, ambrosial dusks and dawns,
Day risen aloft, a multitude of doves –
And, with the naked eye, vouchsafed visions;

Watched horizontal orbs, like spotlights trained
On some barbaric tragedy of old,
Direct their peacock rays along the sun-blind
Waters, and heard their clattering slats unfold.

I dreamed the emerald snow of dazzling chasms,
Kisses ascending to the eyes of the sea,
The circulation of mysterious plasms
And mornings loud with phosphorous harmony.

Trembling, I heard volcanic eructations,
A thrash of behemoths . . . But now, my ears
Weary of this crescendo of sensations,
I thought of Europe and her ancient towers.

Delirious capes! Strewn archipelagoes!
Do you nurse there in your galactic foam
The glistening bodies of obscure flamingoes
Tranced in a prescience of the life to come?

Meuse of the cloud-canals, I would ask of you
Only the pond where, on a quiet evening,
An only child launches a toy canoe
As frail and pitiful as a moth in spring.

A Garage in Co. Cork

Surely you paused at this roadside oasis
In your nomadic youth, and saw the mound
Of never-used cement, the curious faces,
The soft-drink ads and the uneven ground
Rainbowed with oily puddles, where a snail
Had scrawled its slimy, phosphorescent trail.

Like a frontier store-front in an old western
It might have nothing behind it but thin air,
Building materials, fruit boxes, scrap iron,
Dust-laden shrubs and coils of rusty wire,
A cabbage-white fluttering in the sodden
Silence of an untended kitchen garden.

Nirvana! But the cracked panes reveal a dark
Interior echoing with the cries of children.
Here in this quiet corner of Co. Cork
A family ate, slept, and watched the rain
Dance clean and cobalt the exhausted grit
So that the mind shrank from the glare of it.

Where did they go? South Boston? Cricklewood?
Somebody somewhere thinks of this as home,
Remembering the old pumps where they stood,
Antique now, squirting juice into a chrome
Lagonda or a dung-caked tractor while
A cloud swam on a cloud-reflecting tile.

Surely a whitewashed sun-trap at the back
Gave way to hens, wild thyme, and the first few
Shadowy yards of an overgrown cart-track,
Tyres in the branches such as Noah knew –
Beyond, a swoop of mountain where you heard,
Disconsolate in the haze, a single blackbird.

Left to itself, the functional will cast
A death-bed glow of picturesque abandon.
The intact antiquities of the recent past,
Dropped from the retail catalogues, return
To the materials that gave rise to them
And shine with a late sacramental gleam.

A god who spent the night here once rewarded
Natural courtesy with eternal life –
Changing to petrol pumps, that they be spared
For ever there, an old man and his wife.
The virgin who escaped his dark design
Sanctions the townland from her prickly shrine.

We might be anywhere – in the Dordogne,
Iquitos, Bethlehem – wherever the force
Of gravity secures houses and the sun
Selects this fan-blade of the universe
Decelerating while the fates devise
What outcome for the dawdling galaxies?

But we are in one place and one place only,
One of the milestones of earth-residence
Unique in each particular, the thinly
Peopled hinterland serenely tense –
Not in the hope of a resplendent future
But with a sure sense of its intrinsic nature.

The Woods

Two years we spent
down there, in a quaint
outbuilding bright with recent paint.

A green retreat,
secluded and sedate,
part of a once great estate,

it watched our old
bone-shaker as it growled
with guests and groceries through heat and cold,

and heard you tocsin
meal-times with a spoon
while I sat working in the sun.

Above the yard
an old clock had expired
the night Lenin arrived in Petrograd.

Bourbons and Romanovs
had removed their gloves
in the drawing-rooms and alcoves

of the manor house;
but these illustrious
ghosts never imposed on us.

Enough that the pond
steamed, the apples ripened,
the conkers on the gravel opened.

Ragwort and hemlock,
cinquefoil and ladysmock
throve in the shadows at the back;

beneath the trees
foxgloves and wood-anemones
looked up with tearful metamorphic eyes.

We woke the rooks
on narrow, winding walks
familiar from the story books,

or visited
a disused garden shed
where gas-masks from the war decayed;

and we knew peace
splintering the thin ice
on the bath-tub drinking-trough for cows.

But how could we
survive indefinitely
so far from the city and the sea?

Finding, at last,
too creamy for our taste
the fat profusion of that feast,

we travelled on
to doubt and speculation,
our birthright and our proper portion.

Another light
than ours convenes the mute
attention of those woods tonight –

while we, released
from that pale paradise,
ponder the darkness in another place.

The Earth

(after Pasternak)

Spring bursts in our houses.
The moth of winter quits
Its hiding-place and flits
Into the light of day
To gasp on cotton blouses;
Fur coats are locked away.

The cactus shakes itself
And stretches in its pot;
Attic and dusty shelf
Inhale the open air.
This is the time for twilit
Trysts beside the river,

Time for the injudicious
Out-in-the-open voices
And gossip like thaw-water
Dropping from the eaves.
Sob stories and laughter
Dance in the woken leaves.

Outside and in, the same
Mixture of fire and fear,
The same delirium
Of apple-blossom at
Window and garden gate,
Tram stop and factory door.

So why does the dim horizon
Weep, and the dark mould
Resist? It is my chosen
Task, surely, to nurse
The distances from cold,
The earth from loneliness.

Which is why, in the spring,
Our friends come together
And the vodka and talking
Are ceremonies; that the river
Of suffering may release
The heart-constraining ice.

The Globe in North Carolina

'There are no religions, no revelations;
   there are women.'
            – VOZNESENSKY, *Antiworlds*

The earth spins to my finger-tips and
Pauses beneath my outstretched hand;
White water seethes against the green
Capes where the continents begin.
Warm breezes move the pines and stir
The hot dust of the piedmont where
Night glides inland from town to town.
I love to see that sun go down.

It sets in a coniferous haze
Beyond Tennessee; the Anglepoise
Rears like a moon to shed its savage
Radiance on the desolate page,
On Dvořák sleeves and Audubon
Bird-prints. An electronic brain
Records the concrete music of
Our hardware in the heavens above.

From Hatteras to the Blue Ridge
Night spreads like ink on the unhedged
Tobacco fields and clucking lakes,
Bringing the lights on in the rocks
And swamps, the farms and motor courts,
Substantial cities, kitsch resorts –
Until, to the mild theoptic eye,
America is its own night-sky,

Its own celestial fruit, on which
Sidereal forms appear, their rich
Clusters and vague attenuations
Miming galactic dispositions.
Hesperus is a lighthouse, Mars
An air-force base; molecular cars
Arrowing the turnpikes become
Lost meteorites in search of home.

No doubt we could go on like this
For decades yet; but nemesis
Awaits our furious make-believe,
Our harsh refusal to conceive
A world so different from our own
We wouldn't know it were we shown.
Who, in its halcyon days, imagined
Carthage a ballroom for the wind?

And what will the new night be like?
Why, as before, a partial dark
Stage-lit by a mysterious glow
As in the *Night Hunt* of Uccello.
Era-provincial self-regard
Finds us, as ever, unprepared
For the odd shifts of emphasis
Time regularly throws up to us.

Here, as elsewhere, I recognize
A wood invisible for its trees
Where everything must change except
The fact of change; our scepticism
And irony, grown trite, be dumb
Before the new thing that must come
Out of the scrunched Budweiser can
To make us sadder, wiser men.

Out in the void and staring hard
At the dim stone where we were reared,
Great mother, now the gods have gone
We put our faith in you alone,
Inverting the procedures which
Knelt us to things beyond our reach.
Drop of the oceans, may your salt
Astringency redeem our fault!

Veined marble, if we only knew,
In practice as in theory, true
Salvation lies not in the thrust
Of action only, but the trust
We place in our peripheral
Night garden in the glory-hole
Of space, a home from home, and what
Devotion we can bring to it!

. . . You lie, an ocean to the east,
Your limbs composed, your mind at rest,
Asleep in a sunrise which will be
Your mid-day when it reaches me;
And what misgivings I might have
About the true importance of
The merely human pale before
The mere fact of your being there.

Five miles away a south-bound freight
Shrieks its euphoria to the state
And passes on; unfinished work
Awaits me in the scented dark.
The halved globe, slowly turning, hugs
Its silence, and the lightning bugs
Are quiet beneath the open window
Listening to that lonesome whistle blow. . .